CW01455583

Para-Site Publications

Copyright © 2008 Lydia Fraser-Ward and Tamara von Werthern

Lydia Fraser-Ward and Tamara von Werthern have asserted their moral right
to be identified as the authors of this work

'Para-Site: The First Five Years' first published in Great Britain in 2008 as a hardback original by
Para-Site Publications, 162a Amhurst Road, London E8 2AZ

Photography by Christian Schmermer www.schmermer.com
Typeset and designed by Richard Clark
Printed and bound in Great Britain by Biddles Ltd, King's Lynn, Norfolk
A CIP catalogue record for this book is available from the British Library

ISBN 978-0-9559511-0-7

Contents

PARA-SITE

THE FIRST FIVE YEARS

Lydia Fraser-Ward
Tamara von Werthern

Para-Site Publications

DEDICATED TO

EMILIO ROMERO

Foreword

I CANNOT CLAIM TO HAVE SEEN EVERY ONE OF THE SHOWS DOCUMENTED IN THIS BOOK. BUT I HAVE SQUATTED (THE WORD IS APPROPRIATE) IN A PUBLIC LAVATORY IN KINGSTON-UPON-THAMES; I HAVE STOOD AMIDST TRENDY ART MARKETEERS IN A HUGE MARQUEE IN REGENT'S PARK; AND I HAVE BEEN MESMERISED IN A WHITECHAPEL ART GALLERY BY THE INTERRUPTION OF THREE GORGEOUS IF SATANIC-LOOKING WOMEN APPARENTLY BLIND TO THE THRONG OF GALLERY-GOERS THROUGH WHOM THEY MADE THEIR IMPERIOUS PROGRESS.

YOU HAVE TO BE PREPARED FOR ANYTHING AT A PARA-SITE SHOW, BUT WHAT YOU DON'T HAVE TO BE IS ON THE DEFENSIVE. FOR ALL THEIR EXPERIMENTALISM PARA-SITE SEEM TO ME TO BE ESSENTIALLY BENIGN: THEY LIKE PLAYING GAMES BUT NOT AT THE EXPENSE OF THEIR AUDIENCES.

THIS BOOK THRUMS WITH THAT SENSE OF FUN – AS WELL AS HINTING AT THE RICH AND WEIRD INVENTIVENESS THAT IS PARA-SITE'S STOCK-IN-TRADE.

SO, SEE YOU AT THE NEXT EXTRAORDINARY VENUE!

NICK HERN

JUNE 2008

Introduction

FIVE YEARS OF PARA-SITE, SEVEN SHOWS AND
TWENTY-FIVE PARTICIPANTS WHO HAVE HELPED US
PERFORM IN UNUSUAL SPACES ACROSS THE UK IS A
REASON TO CELEBRATE, TO LOOK BACK OVER OUR
WORK TO DATE AND FIND INSPIRATION IN THESE
PAGES FOR OUR FUTURE.

WE HOPE YOU WILL ENJOY WHAT WE HAVE PUT
TOGETHER IN THIS BOOK. SOME OF YOU WILL HAVE
FOLLOWED US ALONG THE WAY AND WE HOPE YOU
WILL CONTINUE TO DO SO AND JOIN US AS OUR
JOURNEY CONTINUES.

WE HAVE HAD A LOT OF FUN, SLEEPLESS NIGHTS,
TEARS AND TANTRUMS TO GET WHERE WE ARE TODAY
AND WE HOPE THIS IS REFLECTED HERE. THE SPACES
WHICH HAVE INFORMED ALL OUR PIECES SO FAR ARE
DIVERSE AND STRANGE, BUT HUGELY INSPIRING.
THEY HAVE MOVED OUR PRACTICE ON AND CONTINUE
TO DO SO.

WE LIKE TO TELL STORIES, FIND CHARACTERS IN
THE ATMOSPHERE OF EACH PLACE WE WORK IN AND
TRANSLATE THESE WITH DANCE, ACTING AND PHYSICAL
THEATRE WITH HELP FROM MAKE-UP, MUSIC, LIGHT
AND PROJECTION — ANYTHING THAT SERVES THE
PARTICULAR SPACE WE FIND OURSELVES IN.

IT IS WITH NOT A LITTLE PRIDE THAT WE NOW
LIKE TO REFLECT ON THIS JOURNEY AND WE WANT TO
INVITE YOU TO COME WITH US AND BE AS INSPIRED
AS WE ARE BY THE POSSIBILITIES INHERENT IN
PLACES WHICH YOU NORMALLY JUST PASS BY.

LYDIA FRASER-WARD & TAMARA VON WERTHERN
PARA-SITE CO-ARTISTIC DIRECTORS

Missing Out

THE TOILET GALLERY — MARCH 2004

"I WELL REMEMBER PARA-SITE AND THEIR PRODUCTION OF 'MISSING OUT'. ALTHOUGH WE HAVE HAD MANY MEMORABLE EVENTS IN THE TOILET GALLERY, FROM OUR OPENING NIGHT WITH GILBERT & GEORGE CHRISTENING THE SPACE TO SPENDING A WEEK MYSELF 'LOCKED IN' THE TOILET GALLERY, I HAVE TO SAY THE EVENT I HAVE THE FONDEST MEMORIES OF IS THE TIME PARA-SITE SPENT IN RESIDENCY IN OUR TINY SPACE. I THINK I CAME ALONG FOR FIVE PERFORMANCES TRYING TO BRING AS MANY OF MY COLLEAGUES AND FRIENDS ALONG TO THIS EXTRAORDINARY EVENT.

EACH NIGHT 'MISSING OUT' WAS PERFORMED WITH REAL ATTENTION TO DETAIL AND INTIMACY WITH THE AUDIENCE. THE THREE TALENTED ACTORS WHO WERE PARA-SITE VERY QUICKLY MADE A NAME FOR THEMSELVES WITHIN KINGSTON AND PROVIDED RESIDENTS WITH A UNIQUE OPPORTUNITY TO WITNESS A YOUNG, VIBRANT COMPANY AT THE VERY BEGINNING OF THEIR ROAD TO SUCCESS.

I CAN SEE THEM NOW AND HEAR THEM PERFORMING AS IF IT WERE YESTERDAY. IT WAS PROBABLY THE BEST EVER USE OF OUR SPACE - INVENTIVE, WITTY, POIGNANT AND ULTIMATELY PROFOUND; PARA-SITE WERE A FORCE TO BE RECKONED WITH, I AM SO PLEASED WE WELCOMED THEM INTO OUR TINY TOILET."

PAUL STAFFORD - CURATOR, THE TOILET GALLERY

PARA SITE

"Missing Out"
MARCH 4 - 26.
Wed - Fri 7pm   Sat 3 + 5pm
Sun 4pm book 0790419 3166

THE TOILET GALLERY
WE RE-CYCLE
143/159 CLARENCE STREET
KINGSTON - LONDON
TEL: 07881832291
e-mail: p.stafford@kingston.ac.uk

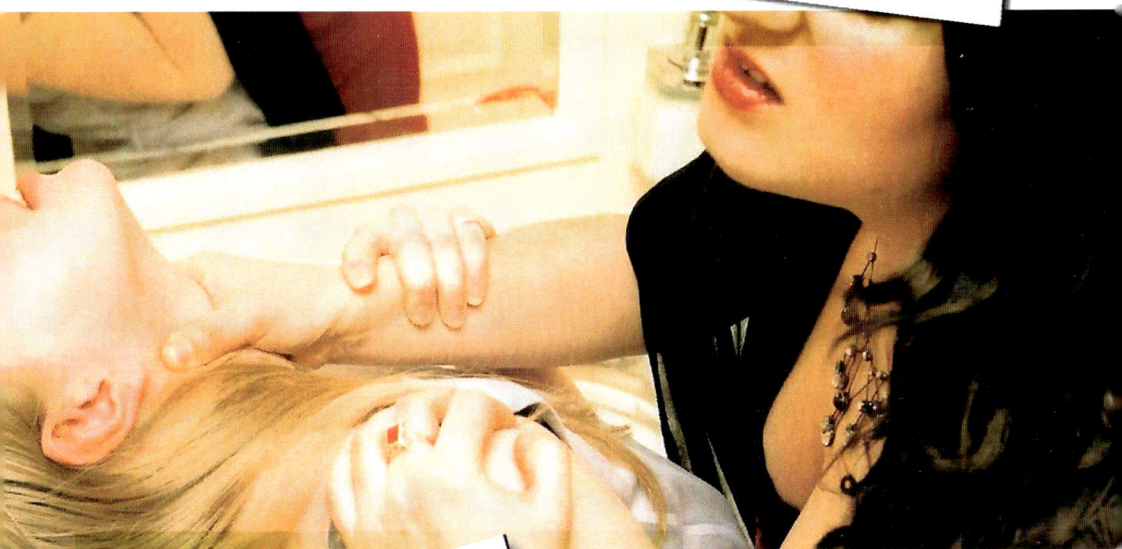

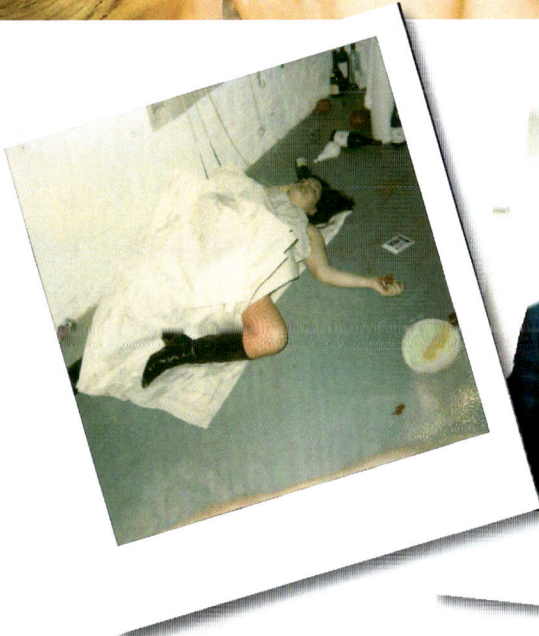

13

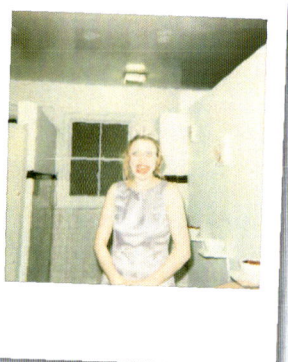

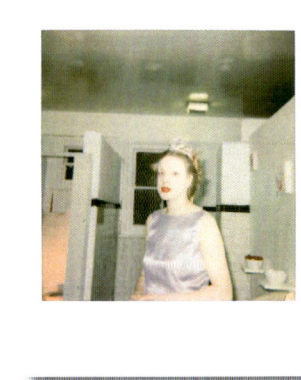

THERE'S A MAN IN HIGH HEELS SHAVING HIS LEGS.
HE LIVES HERE.

MUSIC THUDS FROM THE ROOM NEXT DOOR. SYLVIA IS
WAITING TO MEET A BLIND DATE WHO NEVER SHOWS. SHE
SEEKS SOLACE IN PRAYER IN ONE OF THE CUBICLES.

JENNY JUST WANTS TO HAVE FUN

BUT NOBODY SHOWS UP TO HER BIG BASH AND THERE'S A
BETTER RECEPTION IN THE TOILETS...

15

Love-struck!

SYLVIA STILL HASN'T FOUND HER MAN.

NOW SHE SEARCHES AN ART GALLERY FOR
SENSITIVE, CULTURALLY-INTERESTED MR PERFECT.

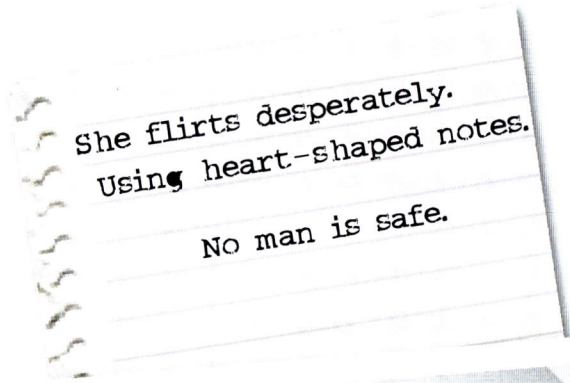

She flirts desperately.
Using heart-shaped notes.

No man is safe.

MEET ME AT THE
TOILETS

IS THAT YOUR
MOTHER OR YOUR
GIRLFRIEND?
I LOVE YOU
MORE

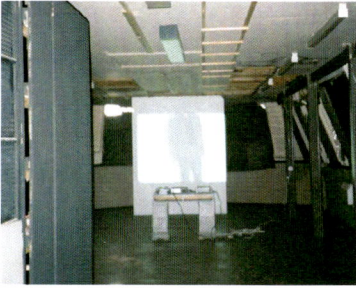

THE POSTAL ROOM
WEEKEND
JUNE 5th-6th 2004

Waygood Gallery and Studios, 2nd Floor
39 High Bridge, Newcastle Upon Tyne, NE1 1EW UK

Saturday 5th June 2004 1pm - 10pm & Sunday 6th June 2004 1pm - 5pm
As part of Waygoods current exhibition RETURN TO SENDER you are invited to a weekend of contemporary Fluxus events including
mail art, live art and film. The Postal Room will be open for all mail art business, including beginning and sending your own mail
works, viewing all correspondence received to date and taking part in live mail art projects.

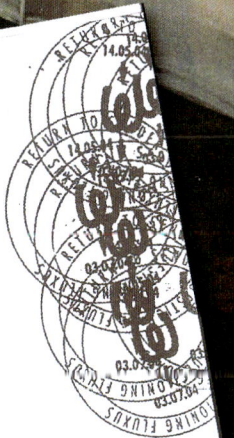

WHEN SHE TRIPS OVER AND FALLS
FLAT ON HER FACE, SPILLING THE
CONTENTS OF HER HANDBAG, IT'S
TIME FOR A TRIP TO THE TOILETS
WHERE SHE ANALYSES THE PITFALLS
OF MODERN LOVE.

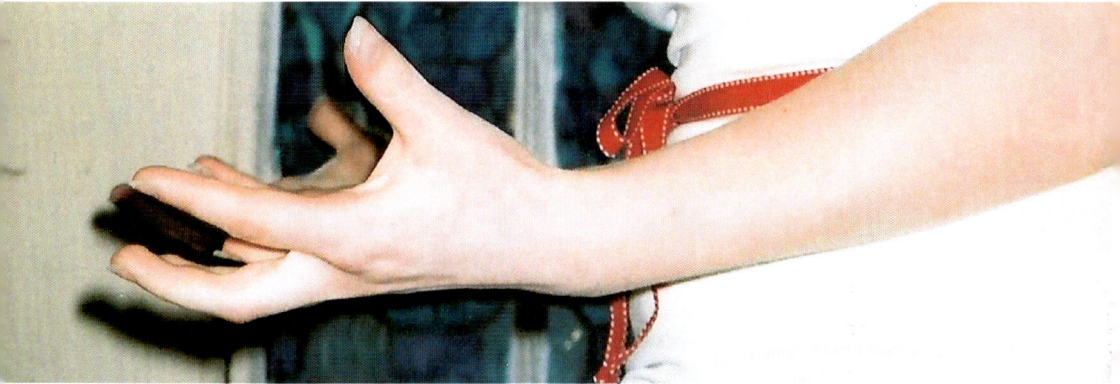

"I WENT SHOPPING. I CHANGED MY WHOLE WARDROBE. I BOUGHT
NEW BOOKS, FOR INNER VALUES. I HAVE SYSTEMATICALLY
LOOKED FOR THE RIGHT PLACES TO MEET THE RIGHT SORT
OF MEN. I DID CHURCHES. I DID SUPERMARKETS. I EVEN
TRIED THE LIBRARY. BUT NOW I REALLY THINK I HAVE FOUND
THE IDEAL SETTING. THE ART GALLERY. OKAY, 50% ARE
GAY, I GRANT YOU THAT. BUT THE OTHER HALF: CULTURALLY
INTERESTED, SENSITIVE, PROBABLY GOOD WITH CHILDREN,
LITERATE, INTERESTING, FUNNY HAIR."

LOVE-STRUCK! 2004

Offstage

"THAT'S IT, NOW AS YOU'RE STRETCHING OUT STILL, I REALLY WANT YOU TO FEEL LIKE A CREATURE THAT IS ALIVE, A SORT OF ANIMAL, CRAWLING THROUGH THE SPACE. GET GROUNDED NOW AS YOU CRAWL AND I WANT YOU TO FEEL AS IF YOUR ENERGY IS PUSHING THROUGH YOUR LIMBS AND OUT INTO THE WORLD! YES! LIKE A BEAM OF LIGHT IS COMING OUT OF YOUR PAWS... AND OUT OF YOUR HEAD — AND OUT OF YOUR MOUTH... AND OUT OF YOUR ANUS!! OK, AND NOW RELAX."

OFFSTAGE 2004

ONLY THE LEADING MAN IS
CONFIDENT OF THEATRICAL
SUCCESS.

HIS SISTER, A LAST-
MINUTE REPLACEMENT,
RESENTS HAVING TO WEAR
A BEARD.

AND THE LEADING LADY
IS MORE INTERESTED IN
GETTING INTO HIS PANTS
THAN GETTING ON STAGE.

REGENT'S PARK
London NW1

FRIEZE ART FAIR

1 DAY PASS

£12.00 (complimentary)

Last entry 1 hour before closing time

Date of Issue:
15-September-2004

www.seetickets.com

Booking Ref:
13612811

Opening Time
11.00am

Closing Time
7.00pm
(5.00pm Monday 18th)

See™

DRAMA CLASSICS

SOPHOCLES

OEDIPUS

"'CHRISTIAN, WE'RE HAVING A SHOW AT THE FRIEZE. CAN YOU TAKE SOME PICTURES FOR US DURING THE PLAY? THE USUAL STUFF, YOU KNOW...'

THAT WAS THE CALL I GOT FROM TAMARA A FEW WEEKS BEFORE THE ART FAIR.

IT WAS SET TO START IN THE AUDITORIUM. NO CURTAIN TO BE LIFTED, JUST A FEW PEOPLE TALKING LOUDER THAN USUAL IN AN OPEN SPACE. THE DIALOGUE WAS MY SIGNAL AND I STARTED WORKING. AS SOON AS THE BYSTANDERS SAW THERE WAS SOMEBODY TAKING PICTURES OF THE ACTORS, THEY REALISED THAT THIS WAS SOMEHOW INTENTIONAL. IT FELT AS IF I WAS SUDDENLY BECOMING PART OF THE PLAY, PROMPTING THE ATTENTION OF THE VIEWERS TO THE NEXT ACTION BY SIMPLY FOCUSING ON THE ACTOR WHOSE TURN IT WAS NEXT."

CHRISTIAN SCHMERMER - PARA-SITE PHOTOGRAPHER

Drive Faster...
We'll Miss It!

SOUTH HILL PARK — MAY 2005

"IN 2005, I MARRIED LYDIA FRASER-WARD. A HAPPY UNION, WE HOPED, BUT, AS IT TURNED OUT, NOTHING SO BECAME OUR LIVES TOGETHER AS OUR LEAVING EACH OTHER. LOUDLY AND PUBLICLY. IN BRACKNELL. AS ART.

WE WEREN'T WILL AND LYDIA, OF COURSE. WE DECIDED TO BE MATT AND SADIE, A YOUNG COUPLE WHOSE SEEMINGLY PLACID RELATIONSHIP CONCEALED A KNOTTY BUNDLE OF ANXIETIES. ESSENTIALLY, WE WERE THE COUPLE THAT SHOULD NEVER HAVE BEEN. AND WE WANTED TO SEE HOW THIS SUBTLY CATASTROPHIC PARTNERSHIP WOULD FARE IF WE ALLOWED IT TO IMPLODE.

LYDIA AND I SPENT MANY AFTERNOONS TOGETHER AS MATT AND SADIE, LIVING LIVES OF DOMESTIC ORDINARINESS. WE'D ALSO TALK AS ACTORS, OF COURSE, AND OFFER SUGGESTIONS TO EACH OTHER. BUT IT WAS INTERESTING HOW THE CORDIAL AND FRIENDLY WORKING RELATIONSHIP LYDIA AND I ENJOYED WAS NOTHING LIKE AS THEATRICALLY CREATIVE AS MATT AND SADIE'S TENSE AND (CLEARLY) DOOMED UNION.

notes on Sadie's Character

s **late** – due to bad judgement on timing, bad luck, forgetfulness

r **find her shoes** – she has lots of pairs, doesn't store them properly.
when it comes to alcohol so often gets drunk

ut **her friends** – especially female ones.
rom long midnight chats

bills are sky high

ex-

tly **an**
arance,
where s.

s **wet to**
ays seem
discomfo
avy sleep

to **travel**
f her, eith
h actually
t, but still f

noia about
o, she canno
her lateness, she is never tota
anaged, with all this practic
hes, shoes, hairstyles – the
ways slightly wrong with th

with
on it

South Hill Park
Fri 27th (from 6.30pm).
Sat 28th (from midday) May

Fresh

so
he
be
d

te **scatty** – to look at and to
icty is bred out of all of these things, but it also makes for great
and although she is often the subject of their mocking, it is in a
ng that she can laugh at her own faults and has to, because she is
task on them everyday by those around her – cause for more

very **chatty** – she can talk insesantly about any subject
ll or boring but

BY THE END OF MAY, WE'D WORKED ON OUR MARRIAGE FOR LONG ENOUGH,
IT WAS TIME TO SEE IT UNRAVEL. PARA-SITE WAS BOOKED FOR THE
VERY FIRST FRESH FESTIVAL AT SOUTH HILL PARK, BUT WE WEREN'T
ON THE BILL AS SUCH. OUR PERFORMANCE WAS TO BE EMBEDDED IN
THE AUDIENCE ITSELF — MATT AND SADIE HAD COME ALONG FOR THE
FESTIVAL AS PUNTERS. IT JUST SO HAPPENED THAT THE COLLAPSE
OF THEIR MARRIAGE WAS TO BE ONE OF THE NUMBERS. BETWEEN EACH
ACT, AUDIENCE NEARBY WERE SURPRISED BY THEIR BEHAVIOUR. MATT
AND SADIE WERE UNABLE TO SPEAK TO EACH OTHER WITHOUT HURT.
AS THEY WALKED BETWEEN SHOWS, ONE WOMAN TUTTED. LOUDLY.

BUT THEIR TIME CAME DURING THE INTERVAL. WE MADE SURE MATT AND SADIE GOT THEMSELVES INTO THE CENTRE OF THE BAR, FROM WHERE TWO FLOORS OF AUDIENCE MEMBERS COULD SEE AND HEAR THEM AND THEN WE LET THE MARRIAGE END. THE ARGUMENT WAS LOUD, TEARFUL, AT ONE POINT CONCILIATORY, BUT ULTIMATELY DESTRUCTIVE.

LOOKING BACK, I CAN'T REMEMBER WHAT LYDIA AND I DECIDED TO ARGUE ABOUT. I REMEMBER EXACTLY MY FEELINGS OF FRUSTRATION, RAGE AND ULTIMATELY FREEDOM AS THE MATT AND SADIE MARRIAGE WAS MERCIFULLY TERMINATED. I REMEMBER EVERYTHING THAT MATT REMEMBERS, IN SHORT. I JUST CAN'T REALLY RECALL WILL.

I ALSO HAVE NO IDEA WHAT THE AUDIENCE THOUGHT OF THE PIECE. WE DIDN'T GO BACK INSIDE AFTER OUR ROW, AND WE CERTAINLY HADN'T TAKEN A BOW. IN FACT, IT HAD ALL FELT PRETTY BLOODY AWFUL. JUST LIKE WE'D PLANNED.

AS AN ACTOR, MAKING MATT AND HELPING TO CONCOCT SADIE WAS A WONDERFUL ACT OF ARTISTIC CREATIVITY. DESTROYING THEIR MARRIAGE IN ONE ACT OF PUBLIC AGGRESSION, AND THEN ALLOWING BOTH CHARACTERS TO SLIP AWAY, FFIT ODDLY CRUEL. SADIE WAS UNSPEAKABLY IRRITATING, BUT I HAD BECOME REALLY FOND OF HER. I THOUGHT ABOUT THEIR UNFORTUNATE LIFE TOGETHER AND FELT THOROUGHLY SORRY FOR THEM."

WILL TOSH – PARA-SITE PERFORMER

On the Edge

STRATFORD CIRCUS — JULY 2006

THERE ARE GLASS
FLOORS, WALKWAYS AND
A THREE-STOREY DROP
IN THE MIDDLE.

SIX WOMEN
TEETERING ON THE
EDGE, ALL LOOKING
FOR SOMETHING,
DESPERATELY TRYING
TO CONNECT.

IF I FALL, WILL
YOU CATCH ME?

WHAT WILL IT TAKE
TO FIND OUT IF YOU
CAN TRULY TRUST
THOSE AROUND YOU?

"SHARING THE SPACE WITH THE AUDIENCE, THE CONTRAST BETWEEN US IN THE SPACE AND THE ARCHITECTURE ITSELF CREATED A TIMELESS EXPERIENCE. I FELT LIKE I'D ALWAYS BEEN THERE, IN THAT UNFAMILIAR SPACE, FLOATING AND BLENDING WITH THE OTHER CHARACTERS' MEMORIES, LOST IN MY OWN MEMORY, UNDISTURBED BY THE CLOSENESS OF THE SPECTATORS."

MARIA RITA SALVI - PARA-SITE PERFORMER

IF I FALL, WILL YOU CATCH ME?

Work, Rest & Play

FIELDGATE GALLERY — APRIL 2007

WHAT IS LEFT AT THE END OF THE DAY, WHEN PARANOIA, GREED AND VIOLENCE TAKE OVER?

A DANCE PIECE WHICH WEAVES THROUGH THE AUDIENCE WHO BECOME IMMOBILE WITNESSES TO AN ACT OF VIOLENCE.

"WORKING WITH PARA-SITE ON 'WORK, REST & PLAY' WAS A
FANTASTIC EXPERIENCE AS A DRAMATURG. SO MANY DIFFERENT
ART FORMS AND STIMULI FED INTO THE CREATIVE PROCESS.
PARA-SITE EMBRACES COLLABORATION, THEY SEEK TO MAKE
WORK UNIQUE TO ITS ENVIRONMENT, ITS PERFORMERS AND
ITS SPECTATORS. IN THIS WAY THEY CONTINUE TO CHALLENGE
THE CONVENTION OF THEATRE AND LIVE ART, DANCE AND
INSTALLATION AND MOST INTERESTINGLY THEY MAKE THE
VENUE AS IMPORTANT AS THE PIECE ITSELF."

ZENA BIRCH - PARA-SITE DRAMATURG & PERFORMER

"RELAX YOUR FACE. BE CALM. STOP YOUR HANDS FROM SHAKING. SOMETHING UNTOWARD. SOMETHING WRONG. SOMETHING FORBIDDEN. I CAN SMELL IT. I CAN FEEL IT. WATCH HER, CAREFULLY."

WORK, REST & PLAY 2007

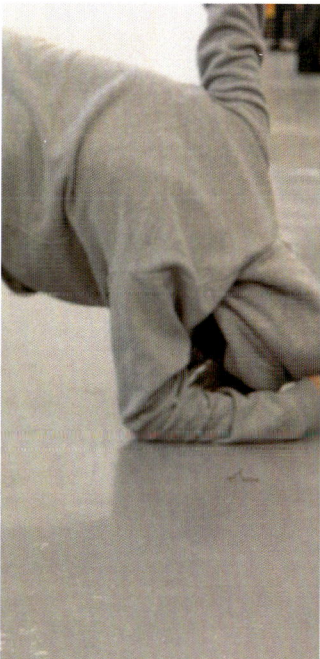

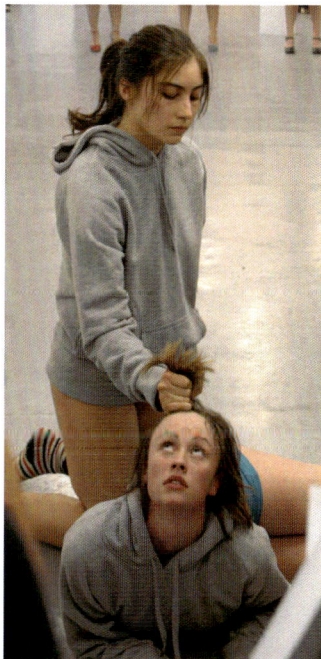

The White Room

TWO MEN LIVE IN A WHITE ROOM ABOVE
A DARK, THREATENING PART OF LONDON.

THEY NEVER LEAVE.

THEY COMFORT EACH OTHER WITH BIZARRE RITUALS,
CHILDISH GAMES AND POT-NOODLES.

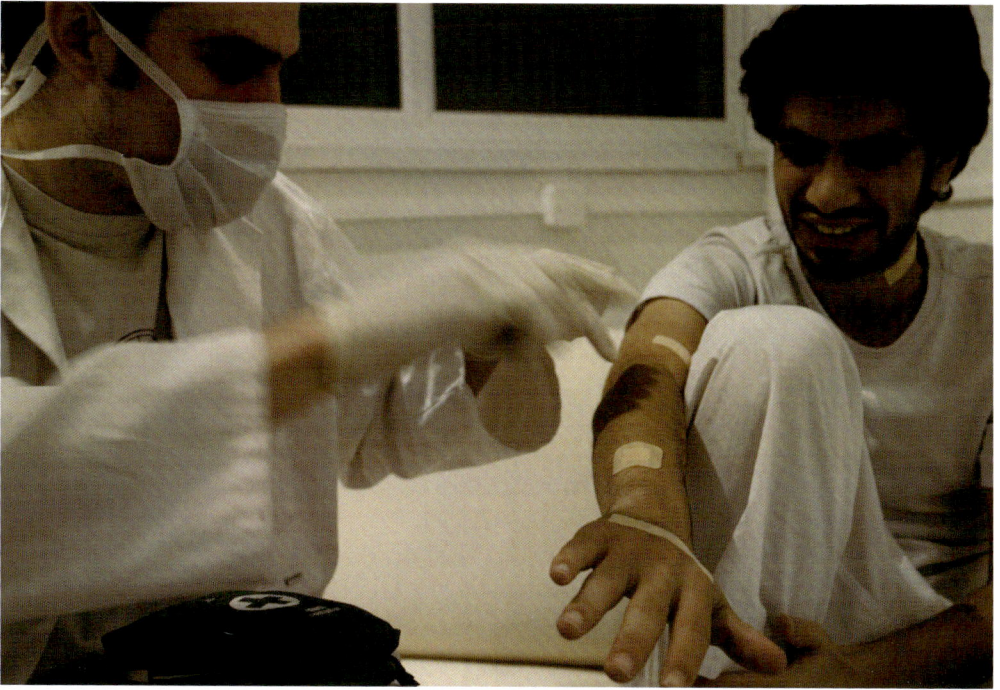

"THE WHITE ROOM WAS ALIVE FOR TWO NIGHTS ONLY. IT WAS CLEAR TO ME THE PERFORMANCE WOULD BE THE BIRTH AND DEATH OF THE PROJECT. AFTER EXPLORING THE SPACE THROUGH IMPROVISATION, GAMES AND RESEARCH OF THEMES LIKE INSOMNIA, MADNESS, INCUBI AND SUCCUBAE, I FELT A GIGER-LIKE CONNECTION IN THAT SOMETHING IN ME, IN MY CHARACTER 'A', IN BEN, TAMARA AND LYDIA, HAD BECOME HYBRID WITH THE SPACE. THIS PIECE WAS BORN LIKE A BUTTERFLY ESCAPING ITS COCOON; AND LIKE THE BUTTERFLY LIVING FOR A DAY, AFTER THE FINAL PERFORMANCE I LOST THE CONNECTION WITH THE SPACE AND LAID IT TO REST.

THIS IS WHY IT WAS A UNIQUE PERFORMANCE FOR ME AND A UNIQUE EXPERIENCE WORKING WITH PARA-SITE. FOCUSING ON THE SPACE IN WHICH WE PERFORMED MADE IT IMMEDIATE AND VALUABLE IN ITS ONENESS AND ITS LIMITATION. I DISCOVERED MANY THINGS ABOUT MYSELF THROUGH THE CHARACTER 'A', MY NEED FOR CHANGE, AND I LOOK WITH INTRIGUE AS TO WHERE PARA-SITE WILL INVADE NEXT."

AKIN GAZI- PARA-SITE PERFORMER

"YOU START TO SEE THINGS. HEAR THINGS. YOU'RE NOT SURE WHAT'S REAL AND NOT REAL. YOU BEGIN TO QUESTION EVERYTHING – EVEN YOURSELF. FOR ALL I KNOW, NONE OF THIS IS REAL. THIS COULD ALL BE ONE LONG DREAM THAT I JUST CAN'T WAKE UP FROM."

THE WHITE ROOM 2007

"WHAT A WEIRD AND WONDERFUL PLACE THE WHITE ROOM WAS! WHAT A JOURNEY! WHAT A WORLD! WHAT A LOT OF POT NOODLES! BEING INVOLVED IN THIS PROJECT WAS SUCH A FANTASTIC AND REWARDING EXPERIENCE. LITERALLY STARTING WITH A BLANK CANVAS OF A ROOM, IN A FEW SHORT WEEKS, DUE TO INTENSE RESEARCH, HARD GRAFT DEVISING AND LOADS OF FUN, IT WAS TRANSFORMED INTO A DARKLY COMIC TALE OF PHOBIAS, LONELINESS, THE HUMAN CONDITION AND BUBBLE WRAP. THERE WILL ALWAYS BE A PART OF ME SLEEPING UNDER A CLOTHES HORSE."

BEN WATSON – PARA-SITE PERFORMER

Collaborators

CAROLINE ALEXANDER, MATT APPLEWHITE, ALI BAYBUTT, ZENA BIRCH, ROBIN BOOTH, LUCY BRADSHAW, MACARENA CAMPBELL, RICHARD CLARK, TOBY CLARKE, MADELEINE COOK, RAY DOWNING, RUTH OUDMAN, ANNIKA ERIKSON, PIPPA FRASER-WARD, JAMES FREEMAN, AKIN GAZI, JANINE HARRINGTON, LISA HOOD, JEANNINE INGLIS HALL, JENNIFER JIMENEZ, MIRANDA KEELING, RICHARD KINGDOM, MAIA LLOYD, JORGE LOPES RAMOS, DAFNE LOUZIOTI, MERCEDES MARESCA, ILANA MITCHELL, ALEXANDRA PAURI, JAMES PILCH, CORIN RHYS JONES, HELEN RYNNE, CHRIS SAKELLARIDIS, MARIA RITA SALVI, CHRISTIAN SCHMERMER, MATT SMALL, PAUL STAFFORD, SINTA TANTRA, MONICA TEUFEL, WILL TOSH, JESKO VON WERTHERN, YU-CHEN WANG, BEN WATSON, KEA YOUNG

WE WOULD LIKE TO THANK EVERYBODY
WHO HAS SUPPORTED OUR WORK BY
PROVIDING THE SPACE FOR IT TO HAPPEN
AND THE EYES TO SEE IT WITH. MORE
THAN ANYTHING WE'D LIKE TO THANK
ALL OUR PERFORMERS, COLLABORATIVE
ARTISTS AND OUR PHOTOGRAPHER.

WITHOUT YOU, THIS
BOOK WOULD NEVER
HAVE BEEN PUBLISHED.

Lydia Fraser-Ward

I HAVE ALWAYS BEEN INTRIGUED BY HOW MOVEMENT
IS INFLUENCED BY THE SPACE IN WHICH IT
HAPPENS. I LIKE TO EXPERIMENT WITH DANCE AND
PHYSICAL THEATRE TO EXPLORE THE ARCHITECTURAL
CHALLENGES OUR SITES PRESENT.

Tamara von Werthern

I AM INTERESTED IN FINDING A STORY THAT NEEDS TO BE TOLD, IN WRITING A SCRIPT WHICH WILL LIVE IN THE ROOM IT WAS WRITTEN FOR. MY BACKGROUND IS PLAYWRITING AND I LIKE BUILDING CHARACTERS AND PUZZLING OVER MOTIVATION, STORYLINE AND SUBTEXT.

The Future

THE TIME WHEN WE GET MOST EXCITED IS
JUST BEFORE EACH NEW PROJECT. WE'VE HAD
A LOOK AT A POTENTIAL SITE AND WE'VE
BEEN HOOKED. WE START THROWING IDEAS
ABOUT. MOSTLY OUTLANDISH, AMAZING IDEAS
WHICH WILL PROBABLY NEVER BE POSSIBLE
TO REALISE. WE MIGHT HAVE THREE TO SIX
WEEKS AND A SHOESTRING BUDGET, IF THAT.
WE THINK ABOUT WHO WE'VE WORKED WITH
BEFORE AND WHO WOULD BE BEST FOR THIS
PROJECT NOW. WE GET EXCITED ABOUT LOOKING
FOR NEW PEOPLE. WE MAKE FLOOR PLANS,
MEASURE THE SPACE AND THINK ABOUT THE
MUSIC, LIGHT AND TECHNICAL EXTRAVAGANZA
WE PROBABLY CAN'T AFFORD. THEN WE GO
BACK TO THE DRAWING BOARD AND WRITE DOWN
WHAT THE SPACE REMINDS US OF.

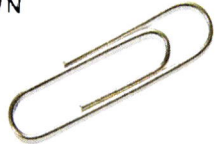

WE HAVE A LOT OF FUN WITH IT BUT
SOMETIMES WE ARE STOPPED SHORT BY HEALTH
AND SAFETY REGULATIONS, PERMISSION ISSUES,
TIME RESTRICTIONS OR WORSE. BUT SOME OF
THESE IDEAS BECOME REAL — THEY CHANGE AND
TAKE SHAPE BECAUSE THEY ARE INFLUENCED
BY THE IDEAS OF OTHERS WHO WE WORK WITH,
UNTIL FINALLY IT BECOMES A PERFORMANCE.
OUR WORK IS EPHEMERAL AND OFTEN DOESN'T
HAVE CRITICS WRITING UP REVIEWS. THERE
WILL NEVER BE A PARA-SITE TRANSFER TO THE
WEST END. IN FACT, YOU'LL BE LUCKY IF YOU
CATCH THE ONE, TWO OR THREE PERFORMANCES
OF EACH PRODUCTION AT ALL. THIS IS WHY
WE HAVE MADE THIS BOOK. SO WE CAN RECORD
OUR WORK AND LOOK BACK AT THE PLACES
WHERE THEATRE CAN HAPPEN, WHERE IT DOES
HAPPEN, AND HOW WE HOPE, IN A SMALL WAY,
WE CONTRIBUTE TO THE WONDERFUL LANDSCAPE
OF LONDON, BY TAKING FROM IT AND ADDING
TO IT, PARASITICALLY.

- what about those funny bull's
eye windows - is there something
behind?

FIVE YEARS OF DOING THIS KIND OF WORK
HAS OPENED OUR EYES TO THE CITY WE LIVE
IN. WE LOOK AT OUR SURROUNDINGS IN A NEW
WAY AND WE THINK ABOUT HOW TO CONTINUE
MAKING THIS WORK HAPPEN. WE VISIT SITES,
PURSUE PEOPLE BEHIND PHONE NUMBERS ON
SIGNS AND FLIRT WITH THE IDEAS THAT WILL
TRANSFORM THESE BUILDINGS STILL STANDING
EMPTY. WE WANT TO GROW BIGGER - IN
PEOPLE, IDEAS AND AUDIENCES. BUT MOST OF
ALL, WE JUST WANT TO KEEP DOING WHAT WE
ARE DOING NOW.

- could we project people's
thoughts over their heads?

Abandoned petrol
station? dri-
Let's have cars
in & out!

Contact

LYDIA FRASER-WARD
TAMARA VON WERTHERN

INFO@PARA-SITETHEATRE.CO.UK

WWW.PARA-SITETHEATRE.CO.UK